Did You Read That?

Bulletin Bloopers & Church Funnies

DERRIC JOHNSON

THOMAS NELSON PUBLISHERS
Nasvhille

Copyright © 2000 by Thomas Nelson, Inc.

Published in Nashville, Tennessee, by Thomas Nelson, Inc.

All rights reserved. Written permission must be secured from the publisher to use or reproduce any part of this book except for brief quotations in critical reviews or articles.

Library of Congress Cataloging-in-Publication Data

Did you read that? / [compiled by] Derric Johnson.
     p.   cm.
   ISBN 0-7852-4515-4
   1. Religion—Humor. I. Johnson, Derric
  PN6231.R4 D53   2000
  230′.002′07082—dc21
                                       99–056232
                                          CIP

Printed in the United States of America
3 4 5 6 7 — 04 03 02 01

WHAT DID THAT SAY?

Have you ever laughed in church? Has someone in Sunday school given a funny response to a question? Has the minister unintentionally mis-poken?

Captured in this book are actual announcements, bulletin typos and misprints, kid's humorous and innocent wordings, and more. A wide variety of contributions from ministers and others. The names have been changed to protect the guilty. Enjoy one of God's great gifts to us . . . laughter.

BULLETIN BLOOPERS

This afternoon there will be a meeting in the South and North ends of the Church. People will be baptized at both ends.

Next Sunday is Easter and Mrs. Anderson will come forward and lay an egg on the altar.

On Sunday a special collection will be taken to help defray the expense of the new carpet. All those wishing to do something on the carpet, come forward and get a piece of paper.

A bean supper will be held Saturday evening in the church basement. Music will follow.

The church choir will begin practice for the Christmas cantata next Wednesday at 7:00 p.m. We have a special need for men's voices, but all parts are welcome.

Tonight's sermon:
WHAT IS HELL?
Come early and listen to
our choir practice.

The sermon this morning:
JESUS WALKS ON THE
WATER

The sermon tonight:
SEARCHING FOR
JESUS

The Low Self-Esteem Support
Group will meet Thursday from
7 to 8:30 p.m.
Please use the back door.

The rosebud on the altar this morning is to announce the birth of David Allen, the sin of Mr. and Mrs. Julius Belser.

The outreach committee has enlisted 25 visitors to make calls on people who are not afflicted with any church.

The Ladies Bible Study will be held Thursday morning at 10. All the ladies are invited to lunch in the Fellowship Hall after the B.S. is done.

Ushers will eat the latecomers.

The audience is asked to remain seated until the end of the recession.

The pastor would appreciate it if the ladies of the congregation would lend him their electric girdles for the pancake breakfast next Saturday morning.

The sermon this morning:
WOMEN IN THE
CHURCH

The closing song:
WISE UP, O MEN
OF GOD

The sermon this morning:
<u>GOSSIP . . . THE SPEAKING</u>
<u>OF EVIL</u>

The closing song:
<u>I LOVE TO TELL THE</u>
<u>STORY</u>

The sermon this morning:
CONTEMPORARY ISSUES #3 . . .
EUTHANASIA

The closing song:
TAKE MY LIFE

The sermon this morning:
PREDESTINATION . . .
WHAT ABOUT HELL?

The closing song:
I'LL GO WHERE
YOU WANT ME TO GO

ANNOINTING OF THE SICK. If you are going to be hospitalized for an operation, contact the pastor. Special prayers also for those who are seriously sick by request.

FINDING THE LOVE OF YOUR LIFE. Practical advice and spiritual perspective for singles looking for a mate every Sunday at 10:45 a.m.

The third verse of "Blessed Assurance" will be sung without musical accomplishment.

CHURCH RUMMAGE SALE.

A good opportunity to get rid of anything not worth keeping but too good to throw away. Don't forget your husband.

A songfest was hell at the Methodist Church Wednesday.

Scouts are saving aluminum cans, bottles and other items to be recycled. Proceeds will be used to cripple children.

Due to the pastor's illness, Wednesday's healing service will be discontinued until further notice.

The Reverend Merriweather spoke briefly, much to the delight of the audience.

The choir invites any member of the congregation who enjoys sinning to join the choir.

The eighth-graders will be presenting Shakespeare's "Hamlet" in the church basement Friday at 7 p.m. The congregation is invited to attend this tragedy.

Bertha Belch, a missionary from Africa, will be speaking tonight at Calvary Memorial Church. Come and hear Bertha Belch all the way from Africa.

Announcement in the church bulletin for a National Prayer and Fasting Conference . . . "The cost for attending the Fasting and Prayer Conference includes meals."

This morning the pastor will preach his farewell message after which the choir will sing *BREAK FORTH INTO JOY.*

Miss Charlene Mason sang *I WILL NOT PASS THIS WAY AGAIN* giving obvious pleasure to the congregation.

The peacemaking meeting scheduled for today has been cancelled due to a conflict.

Next Thursday there will be tryouts for the choir. They need all the help they can get.

Barbara remains in the hospital and needs blood donors for more transfusions. She is also having trouble sleeping and requests tapes of Pastor Jack's sermons.

Next Sunday Mrs. Vinson will be soloist for the morning service. The pastor will then speak on <u>IT'S A TERRIBLE EXPERIENCE</u>.

Found in the church nursery . . . a large red ladies purse.

Peter Matthews, in memory of his wife . . . is donating a loud-speaker to the church.

(Printed on a Cassette)

SERMONS BY REV. HUSSLEBERRY

WARNING

DO NOT PLAY WHILE DRIVING

In some cases this product has

been known to cause

drowsiness and disorientation

Our bylaws specifically state that the will of God cannot be overturned without a 2/3 majority vote.

The Church Board has voted to pray for the Pastor's speedy recovery. The vote was 5 to 4.

Since there was no other new business, the Church Board meeting was adjourned to the parking lot where members said what they really meant.

If Christ returns before the millennium, all books about the Second Coming will be sold at 1/2 price.

WANTED!
CHURCH SECRETARY
Must be overweight, elderly and
surly. Call 358-5503 for
interview with pastor's wife.

For those of you who have children and don't know it . . . we have a nursery downstairs.

The choir will meet at the Larsen home for fun and sinning.

During the absence of our pastor, we enjoyed the rare privilege of hearing a good sermon when J. F. Stubbs supplied our pulpit.

Tuesday at 5. p.m. there will be an ice cream social. All ladies giving milk please come early.

Remember in prayer the many who are sick of our church and community.

The concert held in the Fellowship Hall was a great success. Special thanks are due to the minister's daughter, who labored the whole evening at the piano, which as usual fell upon her.

Smile at someone who is hard to love. Say "Hell" to someone who doesn't care much about you.

Don't let worry kill you . . .
let the church help.

Next Sunday is the family hayride and bonfire at the Fowlers. Bring your own hot dogs and guns. Friends are welcome. Everyone come for a fun time.

The agenda was adopted and the minutes were approved. The financial secretary gave a grief report.

The "Over 60s Choir" will be disbanded for the summer with the thanks of the entire church.

The ladies of the church have cast off clothing of every kind and they can be seen in the church basement Friday afternoon.

The service will close with "Little Drops of Water." One of the men will start quietly and the rest of the congregation will join in.

Wednesday the Ladies Liturgy will meet. Mrs. Jones will sing "Put Me in My Little Bed" accompanied by the Pastor.

Evening Massage at 6:00 p.m.

Stewardship Offertory:
"JESUS PAID IT ALL"

Twenty-two members were present at the church meeting held at the home of Mrs. Marsha Crutchfield last evening. Mrs. Crutchfield and Mrs. Rankin sang a duet, "THE LORD KNOWS WHY."

Offertory solo:
"O Holy Nighty"

Today's sermon: "HOW MUCH CAN A MAN DRINK?" with hymns from a full choir.

Hymn 43: "GREAT GOD, WHAT DO
I SEE HERE?"

Preacher: The Rev. Horace Blodgett

Hymn 47: "HARK! AN AWFUL
VOICE IS SOUNDING."

God is Good!
Dr. Hargraves is better.

There will be a potluck supper with prayer and medication to follow.

The Pastor is on vacation. Massages can be given to the church secretary.

Weight Watchers will meet at 7:30 p.m. at the First Presbyterian Church. Please use the large double doors at the side entrance.

Mrs. Peterson will be entering the hospital this week for testes.

The associate Pastor unveiled the Church's new Tithing Campaign slogan last Sunday: "I UPPED MY PLEDGE . . . UP YOURS."

The closing hymn is "ANGELS WE HAVE HEARD GET HIGH."

Jean Williams will be leading a weight-management series on Wednesday nights. She has used the program herself and has been growing like crazy!

The church is glad to have with us today as our guest minister the Rev. Arthur Green, who has Mrs. Green with him. After the service we request that everyone remain in the sanctuary for the Hanging of the Greens.

Please join us as we show our support for Amy and Alan Cowles in preparing for the girth of their first child.

A singing group called THE RESURRECTION was scheduled to sing at church last Sunday. When the snowstorm kept them from performing, it was announced that the THE RESURRECTION was postponed until a later date.

The music for today's service was all composed by George Frederick Handel in celebration of the 300th anniversary of his birth.

We will close our service this morning by singing together, "God bless America, thru the night with a light from a bulb."

Hymn 312: LEAD ON O KINKY COLONEL.

Join and sing everyone's favorite Christmas carol, WHILE SHEPHERDS WASHED THEIR SOCKS BY NIGHT.

Six-year-old Joey Parks entertained us all by closing our songtime by singing lustily, "He socked me and boxed me with His redeeming glove."

Remember our pastor in prayer. He was on his way to the doctor's with rear end trouble when his universal joint gave way, causing him to have an accident.

Pray for Sister Mary Hall. She is bothered by very close veins.

**Sarah Neal will not be able
to play the piano
for offertory this morning.
She was sick, so her
mother took her to the
doctor and had her shot.**

As we gather garments for the Missionary Closet, please note: Ladies, leave your clothes here on Tuesday morning and spend the afternoon having a good time.

Concerning our menu for Wednesday night suppers please note: Every item may or may not be available at all times and sometimes not at all and other times all the time.

We have added a new support group to our growing list of helpful opportunities: ILLITERATE? Write today for free help.

At last word, Emily Hess is alright. She went to the ER where she was examined, X-rated and sent home.

Pastor Bob was released from the hospital on Tuesday, but is still under the doctor's car for physical therapy.

Bill Williams reports that his knee trouble seems to be better after being admitted to the hospital. On the 2nd day the knee was better and on the 3rd day it disappeared completely.

Remember to pray for Sister Miriam. She is tearful and crying constantly. She also appears to be depressed.

**Please place your donation
in the envelope along with
the deceased person
you want remembered.**

Attend and you will hear an excellent speaker and heave a healthy lunch.

The church will host an evening of fine dining, superb entertainment, and gracious hostility.

Suzie writes that her honeymoon with Pastor Bob has been the thrill of a wifetime.

The topic of discussion for our PROSPECTIVE PARENTS SEMINAR is "Should your little boy be circus sized?"

Pray for Mrs. Edith Barrett. For the past three weeks she has been numb from the toes down.

As far as Brother Brown's physical condition is concerned, the lab reports indicate that he has abnormal lover function.

Art Jones, who was suffering from chest pains, was scheduled to have an electrocardiogram. But took a job as a stockbroker instead.

We want everyone to know that safety is one of our priorities. Driving slowly on church property is a necessity or we may have to install bums on the driveways.

There is joy in heaven over one singer who repents.

We will re-enact the Last Supper and journey to the Garden of Gethsemane on Maundy Thursday, March 29 at 7 p.m. We will strip the altar and sanctuary of all color and symbol. Together we will leave the church bare and in silence.

**And we give you thanks,
O God, for the people of
many cultures and nations;
for the young and old
and muddled-aged.**

On March 16th, the prayer group met at the home of Margaret Weare, who is no longer able to attend church services. What a blessing!

Beginning November 5, Pastor Hodges will lead a six-part series on the book of Genesis. Were Adam and Eve really naked in the Garden? Come and see for yourself.

The correspondence committee will assist with the mailing of the newsletter and stapling of the Annual Report to congregational members.

As the maintenance of the churchyard is becoming increasingly costly, it would be appreciated if those who are willing would clip the grass around their own graves.

A note from the pastor: I shall be away from the church office attending the Yearly Meeting from September 11–14. It will be convenient if parishioners will abstain from arranging to be buried, or from making other calls on me during this time.

Our Ladies Bible Study Group tries to assist in serving a luncheon for the families of church members who have died immediately following the funeral.

The annual church picnic will be held Saturday afternoon. If it rains, it will be held in the morning.

As always, Sister Betty's scalped potatoes were the hit of the church potluck dinner last Friday night.

This Sunday night's lesson is the seventh in Pastor William's series on the Ten Commandments: "Thou shalt not admit adultery."

Tonight the youth choir will be singing, "Joshua Fit the Battle of Geritol."

The Sunday School lesson next week will focus on how Noah got the animals into the ark in pears.

Our All-Church potluck is scheduled for this Sunday night. As usual the big question is . . . what's coming up next?

In response to your questions about the surgery on Bob Matson to remove the tumor from his stomach, we are glad to report that everything came out all right.

The Christmas season is upon us and the choir needs one really base singer.

When you hear gossip . . . the best thing you can do is pry about it.

Crying babies and disruptive children, like good intentions, should be carried out immediately.

Sign in a church bawl room:

We shall not all sleep
but we shall all be changed
in the twinkling of an eye.

Remember the Children's Ministry
Fund Raiser . . . Our kids make
great snacks.

IT'S A MIRACLE DEPARTMENT:
Blind Sister Esther Brown will get a
new kidney from her dad whom
she hasn't seen in years.

THE WEDNESDAY NIGHT DINNER SPECIAL:

Turkey	$3.75
Beef	$3.50
Chicken	$3.25
Children	$2.50

Our Church Book Store announces their Semi-Annual After-Christmas Sale.

With our Senior High Graduation Banquet coming up, the Youth Sponsors are asking the girls to drop their strapless gowns

Art Peters, our church chef, really throws his heart into the Wednesday night suppers.

Political red tape is holding up our new building.

If we are to complete our building program, we must have all financial pledges fulfilled by next Sunday. Let us prey.

Today's Sermon:
The Honest Christian

Choir Special:
Steal Away

The Church dinner was like Heaven.
Many we expected to see were
absent.

Members of the Senior Class are not to pass out until the Pastor finishes preaching.

Bill McKee is improving in the hospital, but he is still in the expensive-care unit.

Please help our young people with their Flea Market. They are starting from scratch.

Benjamin Benson and Jessica Carter were married on October 24 in the Church Sanctuary. Thus ends a friendship that began in their school years.

Mrs. Peter Love will sink and Mrs. Wayne Webber will be at the organ. Mrs. Webber will play, "Throw Out the Lifeline."

Sermon :
The Light of the World

Closing Hymn:
Blest Be the Tie That Blinds

This Sunday our visiting preacher is Dr. Raymond Holder. If you would like to see the other pulpit candidates, you will find them hanging in the foyer.

Choral Worship:
When Jesus Speaks Your Name

Sermon:
Are You Scared?

Choral Anthem:
Jesus, Grant Me This I Pray

Sermon:
Money! Money! Money!

**Sermon:
The Most Hated Man
of Israel**

**Invitation Hymn:
Only Trust Him**

Sermon:
Samson's Head in Delilah's Lap

Invitation Hymn:
Leave It There

The Temperance Committee Meeting will be held in the home of Jim and Judy Schmidt next Thursday evening at 7:30. Drinks will be furnished.

CHURCH FUNNIES

Sunday School Teacher: What do you call the land flowing with milk and honey?

Pupil: Messy!

KID #1: What's the highest number you ever counted to?

KID #2: 5,376.

KID #1: Why did you stop there?

KID #2: The sermon was over.

HE: I have nothing but praise for our new minister.

SHE: Yes . . . I noticed that when the offering plate was passed.

A new member asked the Pastor, "Do you believe in predestination?" The Pastor replied, "I knew you were going to ask me that." "Really?" said the parishioner. "WOW!"

At Sunday morning breakfast, the Pastor sat down with a reddened, dampened tissue on his face. His fifteen-year-old daughter asked, "What happened to you?" He replied, "I was thinking about my sermon and I cut my chin." After the service she walked by and whispered, "Next time . . . think about your chin and cut your sermon."

A little boy was asked to name the first man. He quickly answered, "Adam." Then he was asked to name the first woman. He thought a minute and finally answered, "Madam."

MOTHER: What are you children playing?

CHILDREN: Church.

MOTHER: But people shouldn't whisper in church.

CHILDREN: We know . . . but we're in the choir.

Seven-year-old Joey erupted with a loud whistle during the pastoral prayer. After church his mother scolded him asking, "What ever made you do such a thing?" "I asked God to teach me to whistle . . . and He did just then!"

A four-year-old was praying in church . . .
"And forgive us our trashbaskets as we forgive those who put trash in our baskets.

The Pastor's opening prayer began, "O God, give us clean hearts, give us pure hearts, give us sweethearts . . ." and three ladies in the choir added, "Amen!"

The sanctuary lights were dimmed and the choir came down the aisle carrying lighted candles. A three-year-old girl sitting in church for the first time, began to sing in a loud voice, "Happy Birthday to you, Happy Birthday to you . . . "

BOY: God, how long is a million years to you?

GOD: It's like a single second to you.

BOY: How much is a million dollars to you?

GOD: It's like a single penny to you.

BOY: Well, could I please have one of your pennies?

GOD: Certainly . . . in a second.

PASTOR: You need to join the Army of the Lord!

MAN: I'm already in the Army of the Lord, Pastor.

PASTOR: Then why do I see you only at Christmas and Easter?

MAN: (Whispering) I'm in the Secret Service.

DID YOU READ THAT?

Submit your favorite blooper and win a book or CD-ROM.

Send us your favorite blooper or church story for our next book. If your entry is chosen, we will list your name and your saying and send you a copy of our next *Did You Read That?* book.

All entries will have the opportunity to win a free *"Nelson Electronic Bible Reference Library,"* featuring the best of biblical reference materials on the market.

Please send your entries to:

Thomas Nelson, Inc.
Nelson Reference and Electronic
P.O. Box 141000
Nashville, TN 37214

ATTN: 2216